he returned on or before
date below.

WORLD ENERGY ISSUES ✳

COAL

The Big Polluter?

JIM PIPE

ALADDIN/WATTS
LONDON • SYDNEY

Contents

© Aladdin Books Ltd 2010

Designed and produced by
Aladdin Books Ltd
PO Box 53987
London SW15 2SF

First published in 2010
by Franklin Watts
338 Euston Road
London NW1 3BH

Franklin Watts Australia
Level 17/207 Kent Street
Sydney NSW 2000

Franklin Watts is a division of
Hachette Children's Books,
an Hachette UK company.
www.hachette.co.uk

All rights reserved
Printed in Malaysia

Scientific consultant: Rob Bowden

A catalogue record for
this book is available
from the British Library.

Dewey Classification:
333.8'22

ISBN 978 1 4451 0196 5

What's the Issue?

Coal is one of our oldest and most important energy sources – people have been burning it for over 4,000 years. In the past, coal was used to heat homes. Today it is burnt in power plants and steel plants, producing almost half the world's electricity.

Though coal is plentiful and cheap, it's also the dirtiest fuel of all. Burning coal pollutes the air with toxic chemicals and creates mountains of solid waste. It also pumps large amounts of carbon dioxide into the atmosphere, a gas that adds to global warming. If coal is going to remain an important fuel, it needs to clean up its act. An effective way of collecting and storing the carbon dioxide given off needs to be found – and fast. In another 20 years, the damage will already have been done.

◑ Coal Power

A typical coal-fired power plant produces 1,000 MW of electricity, enough for 600,000 homes.

◐ The Human Cost

Coal mining is a dirty, dangerous job. Around the world, thousands of miners are killed each year.

Why Coal?

⚠ Coal Lump

Coal is a hard, black mineral that is mostly found underground. It varies in hardness, colour and the amount of heat it gives off when it burns.

For some, the future of our climate can be summed up in one question: what do we do about coal? It's twice as dirty as natural gas and what we burn now puts more carbon dioxide in the air than all our cars and trucks. So why has it been the world's fastest growing fuel since 2000? Coal is the most plentiful fossil fuel and cheaper than almost all other energy sources. In all, almost 7 billion tonnes of coal are used worldwide each year.

The United States, China, Russia and India all have huge reserves that could last another 150 years or more. Meanwhile, new technologies are being developed to trap carbon dioxide emissions. If successful, coal would probably become the world's most important fuel source.

✦ Burning Coal

Coal is used as a fuel as it burns so well. It burns slowly on the outside and gives off heat for a long time. When it has burnt, all that remains is grey ash.

A Major Energy Source

There was international trade in coal as long ago as the Roman Empire. It provided the energy for the steam engines that created the Industrial Revolution of the 19th century. Using coal to create electricity launched the electric age in the early 20th Century.

Around 50 years ago, oil overtook coal as the world's most important energy source. Yet coal-burning power plants still provide over 45 per cent of the world's electricity and coal is also used in 70 per cent of world steel production.

COAL POWER: For

• Coal is cheap, even compared to other fossil fuels such as oil and gas. A lot of money could be invested in making it cleaner and it would still be competitive.
• Coal is the most widespread fossil fuel.
• World supplies of coal are expected to last another 150 years if used at the current rate.
• Coal can be burned directly or transformed into liquid or gas form.
• New techniques such as coal gasification could unlock huge additional supplies underground.

COAL POWER: Against

• Coal is not a renewable energy source. Once we've burned it all, there isn't any more.
• Coal-fired power plants give off more greenhouse gases that those using gas or oil.
• Burning coal is a major cause of air pollution, including traces of mercury and arsenic that are harmful to health. Plants without scrubbers (page 25) produce sulphur dioxide, creating acid rain.
• Coal mining can be very destructive to the landscape.
• Coal-fired plants generate hundreds of millions of tonnes of solid waste each year, including ash and sludge.

◖ Greenhouse Gases

In an average year, a typical coal plant generates 4 million tonnes of carbon dioxide, the main human cause of global warming. It would take hundreds of millions of mature trees to absorb of all this carbon dioxide.

ENERGY FACTS: A Short History of Coal

2000 BC Ancient peoples burn coal in Europe.
1200 AD Many homes in Britain are heated using coal. In North America, the Hopi people use coal to bake pottery in kilns.
1709 Abraham Darby invents a furnace that uses coke (coal heated in an airtight oven) for smelting iron.
1769 James Watt invents the steam engine, which runs on coal.
1807 First public gas street lights in London – fuelled by the "town gas" made from coal.
1825 George Stephenson invents the first steam train, which burns coal to turn water to steam. Railways soon spread across Europe and America.
1882 Pearl St Plant in New York, the world's first power station, runs on coal.
1950s Many homes still have coal fires that pollute the air of cities like London, causing smog (smoke and fog).
1990s Many US and European coal-fired plants are fitted with scrubbers to clean up the sulphur and nitrogen oxides that cause acid rain.

What Is Coal?

Coal is found on every continent. The oldest coal formed 360-286 million years ago, when a swampy forest of giant ferns covered the land. When these plants died, they piled up in layers. Over time, the weight of the layers above turned the rotting plants into peat.

Over millions of years, heat and pressure caused the peat to turn into a soft material called lignite. Deeper below the surface, the extra pressure created harder coals known as bituminous coal and anthracite. Coal is found in layers called seams. A seam 2 m thick may once have been a 30-m thick layer of peat. Many coal seams are too thin or broken up to be worth mining.

◑ **Fossilised Fern**
Because coal contains the energy from plants that lived millions of years ago, it is called a fossil fuel.

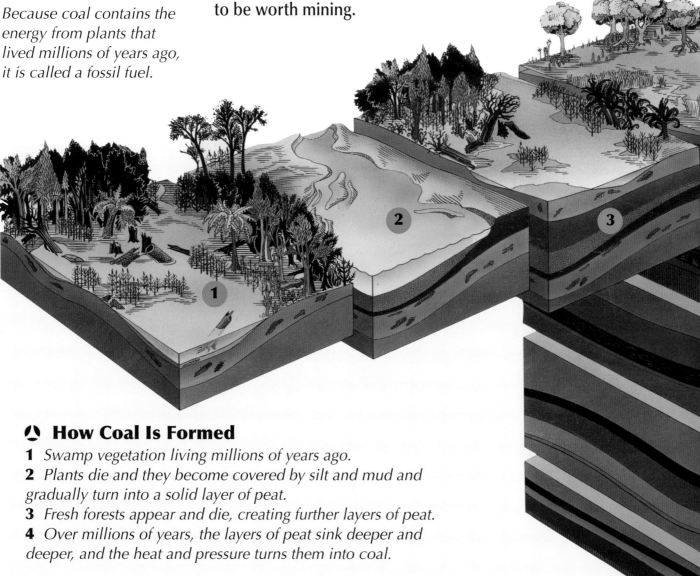

◑ **How Coal Is Formed**
1 *Swamp vegetation living millions of years ago.*
2 *Plants die and they become covered by silt and mud and gradually turn into a solid layer of peat.*
3 *Fresh forests appear and die, creating further layers of peat.*
4 *Over millions of years, the layers of peat sink deeper and deeper, and the heat and pressure turns them into coal.*

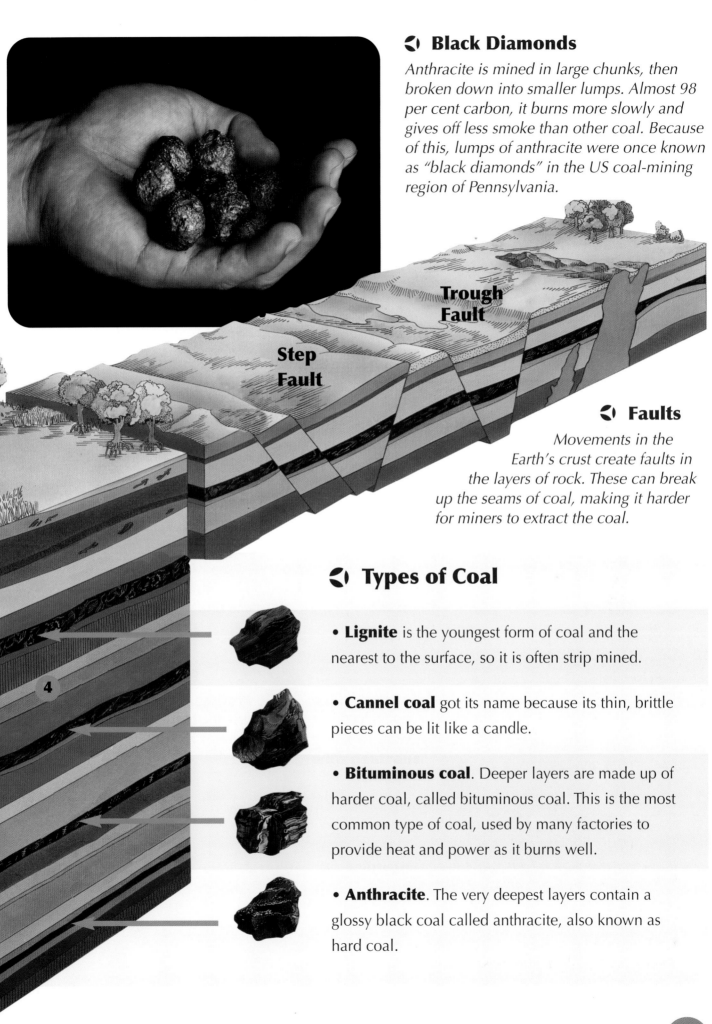

Black Diamonds

Anthracite is mined in large chunks, then broken down into smaller lumps. Almost 98 per cent carbon, it burns more slowly and gives off less smoke than other coal. Because of this, lumps of anthracite were once known as "black diamonds" in the US coal-mining region of Pennsylvania.

Trough Fault

Step Fault

Faults

Movements in the Earth's crust create faults in the layers of rock. These can break up the seams of coal, making it harder for miners to extract the coal.

Types of Coal

- **Lignite** is the youngest form of coal and the nearest to the surface, so it is often strip mined.

- **Cannel coal** got its name because its thin, brittle pieces can be lit like a candle.

- **Bituminous coal**. Deeper layers are made up of harder coal, called bituminous coal. This is the most common type of coal, used by many factories to provide heat and power as it burns well.

- **Anthracite**. The very deepest layers contain a glossy black coal called anthracite, also known as hard coal.

Mining Coal

◐ Finding Coal

Geologists look for underground seams of coal by setting off explosions. These cause shock waves that travel through the rock and back to the surface. Here sensors pick up the echoes and form a map of underground rocks.

When a seam of coal is found, a drilling rig removes rods of rock from under the ground and the samples are tested. If good quality coal is found and it's easy to extract, a mine is sunk.

Today, most miners use machines to remove coal from the ground. Some coal seams are near the surface, while others can be as deep as 1,300 m underground. When coal is mined underground, the seams are connected to the surface via shafts. Lifts take men and equipment down and bring coal back to the surface. Coal is cut from faces that are linked by underground tunnels.

In recent years, many underground mines have been equipped with very powerful automated cutting machines. Steel supports hold up the roof above the machine and its operators. The coal is then carried on conveyor belts to the mine shaft where it is put in skips and taken to the surface.

◑ Cutting Edge

The spinning teeth of this longwall shearer cut into the seam. Then the coal is carried away on a conveyor belt.

Open-Cast Mining

When a coal seam lies within 200 m of the surface it can be dug out. The top layers of soil and rock, the overburden (up to 65 m thick), are broken by explosives and drills, then removed. The coal underneath is scooped up by massive diggers and excavators, then loaded onto trucks or conveyor belts that take the coal out of the mine.

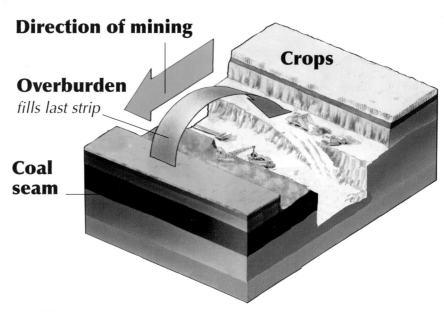

Direction of mining

Crops

Overburden
fills last strip

Coal seam

⚫ Strip Mining

Open-cast mining takes place on a huge scale: whole villages have been destroyed and rebuilt to make way for the giant machinery. A method known as strip mining limits the damage. Once the mining is finished, the dirt and rock are returned to the pit, the topsoil is replaced, and the area is replanted.

ENERGY FACTS: Underground Danger

• Mining is still one of the world's most dangerous jobs. There's the risk of suffocation, gas poisoning, the roof collapsing and flooding.

• The worst disasters are usually caused by methane gas explosions. In April 2010, 29 miners were killed by a blast at the Upper Big Branch mine, West Virginia, USA.

• Sometimes layers of rock shift below the ground, making the floor heave upward. Such a "bump", or "squeeze", can trap miners inside the mine.

⚫ Super Scooper
A bucket wheel excavator can weigh over 13,000 tonnes. It has rotating toothed buckets that can scoop out 240,000 tonnes of coal in a single day – enough to fill 2,400 wagons.

Transporting Coal

Millions of tonnes of coal are transported around the world each day. Coal is heavy and bulky to carry so it's too expensive to move it by road or air. Most is carried off in trains which run between the mines and the power stations or steelworks that use the coal as fuel.

In countries with good river or canal networks, such as China, coal is often carried in barges. Coal is also shipped overseas from mines in Australia to countries in Asia and Europe. A typical ship carries 60,000 tonnes of coal or more in one load. In the United States, giant pipelines carry a mix of coal and water hundreds of kilometres.

⛟ Barges on the Rhine
Rivers such as the Rhine in Germany are packed with barges carrying coal inland. Some barges weigh up to 2,000 tonnes. They are usually loaded by automatic conveyor belts.

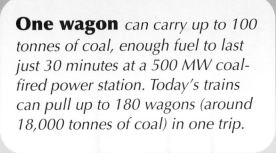

One wagon *can carry up to 100 tonnes of coal, enough fuel to last just 30 minutes at a 500 MW coal-fired power station. Today's trains can pull up to 180 wagons (around 18,000 tonnes of coal) in one trip.*

⊽ Shuttle Train

Coal trains travel at a slow, steady pace because the coal is so heavy. The E60 locomotives on the Black Mesa & Lake Powell railroad (below) are designed for moving coal and spend their life shuttling between mines and the coal user.

In the UK, merry-go-round (MGR) trains are designed to be loaded and unloaded while the train is still on the move. Such trains have a speed device so they travel at a fixed, slow speed during loading/unloading.

◁ Coal Preparation

Coal arriving at a power plant is sorted by size and cleaned, ready for use. Coal straight from the mines often contains soil, rocks and polluting chemicals such as sulphur that need to be removed before it is burnt. The coal is crushed into smaller pieces less than 5 cm big so it can be handled more easily. It is then fed into tanks. These contain a liquid that causes the coal to float, while unwanted rock particles sink to the bottom so they can be removed.

Electricity from Coal

Over half of the world's coal ends up in power stations and is burnt to generate electricity. Over 80 per cent of China's electricity is produced by coal-fired power plants, and it uses more coal than any other nation, followed by the United States (50 per cent of electricity), Russia and India.

The rise in oil prices and the expense of building nuclear plants means there are now an estimated 130 new coal-fired plants being planned around the world.

◑ **Giant Turbine** – *A modern coal-fired plant produces some 1,000 MW of electricity, enough to power 600,000 European homes.*

◔ How It Works

1 The coal is carried into the power station by conveyor belts from which it falls into the pulverising mill.

2 Here the coal is crushed into dust as this makes it burn more fiercely.

3 The coal is then blown by powerful jets of hot air into the boilers, where it burns in towering flames up to 40 m high – that's as high as a ten-storey building.

4 Inside each boiler, water (shown in blue) is turned into steam in reinforced steel tubes and heated until it is white hot.

5 The steam (shown in purple) is then released into the turbine at enormous pressure. It makes the turbine blades spin rapidly.

6 The turbine blades are connected to a shaft that turns a generator, producing electricity.

7 The electricity created is then fed into the national grid along power lines.

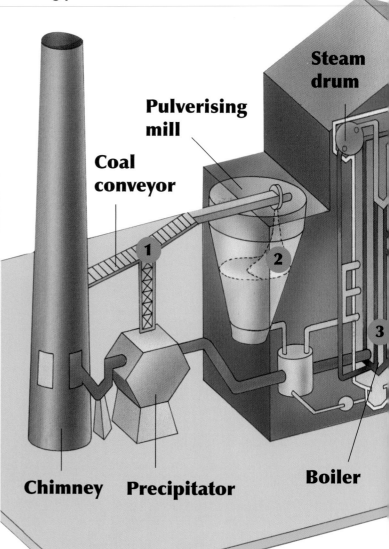

Steam drum

Pulverising mill

Coal conveyor

Chimney   Precipitator   Boiler

◀ Cooling Down, Cleaning Up

In the cooling towers, steam from the condenser is cooled by air from below. The steam condenses (turns into water) and is collected at the bottom. It is then fed back into the condenser to cool spent turbine steam.

After the coal is burnt, all that is left is a grey ash. This has to be removed from coal-fired boilers, although some coal ash can be recycled for building materials. A precipitator also collects particles of dust from the smoke given off by the burning coal.

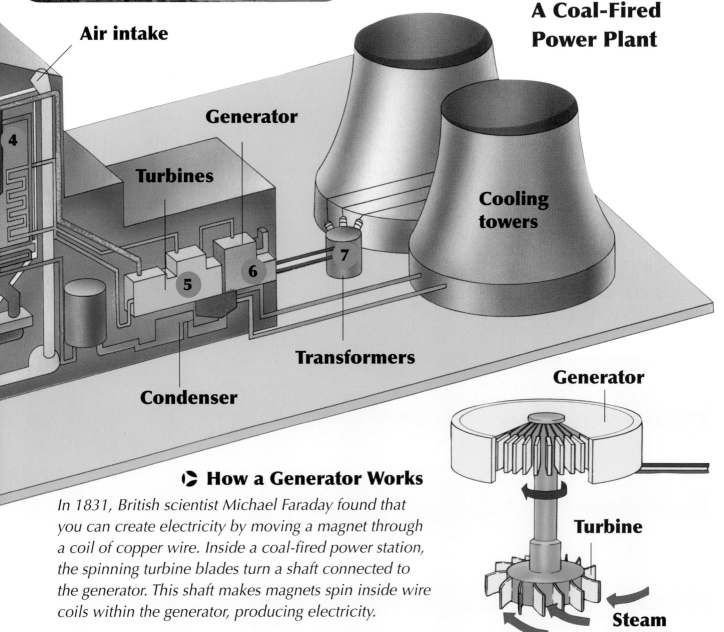

A Coal-Fired Power Plant

Air intake

Generator

Turbines

4

Cooling towers

5

6

7

Condenser

Transformers

Generator

▶ How a Generator Works

In 1831, British scientist Michael Faraday found that you can create electricity by moving a magnet through a coil of copper wire. Inside a coal-fired power station, the spinning turbine blades turn a shaft connected to the generator. This shaft makes magnets spin inside wire coils within the generator, producing electricity.

Turbine

Steam

Coal At Work

◭ Coke in Space

Coke was used for making the heat shields on NASA's Apollo programme space vehicles and on the Mars Pathfinder vehicle.

Coal has many other important uses. There would be no steel industry without coke (coal heated to high temperatures in airtight furnaces) and coal is also used to manufacture cement, aluminium and paper products.

Refined coal tar is used in the manufacture of chemicals, such as creosote and benzene, while the ammonia gas recovered from coke ovens is used to make ammonia salts, nitric acid and fertilisers. Thousands of other goods use coal or its by-products: including soap, aspirin, solvents, dyes, plastics and fibres.

Coke and Steel

In a steel mill, bituminous coal is heated up to 2000°C without air, then sprayed with cold water. This burns off the smoky coal gas and coal tar, turning the coal into coke, which is almost pure carbon. The very high temperatures created by burning coke gives steel the strength and flexibility for things like bridges, buildings and cars. The coke also removes oxygen from the iron ore and allows hot gases to escape.

◖ How Steel is Made

1 *Coke and iron ore (the rock that contains iron) are heated in a blast furnace.*
2 *The white-hot coke reacts with the iron to form molten slag.*
3 *The slag then mixes with the carbon in limestone to make steel.*
4 *Each time the furnace is "tapped", the steel runs off in a fiery liquid stream. It is cast into shapes which harden as it cools.*

Molten Steel

⬣ Cement

The cement used to bind bricks together is one of our most important building materials. Over 2.7 billion tonnes of cement are manufactured each year, and most cement kilns use coal as fuel. As a result, the cement industry produces about 5 per cent of the world's major greenhouse gas, carbon dioxide.

Home Fuel

A century ago, most homes were heated with coal fires, but at a terrible cost. The notorious London smog, which used to kill hundreds of people, was based on coal smoke. As a result, few Americans or Europeans still have coal fires.

Health Hazard

Coal is still a very popular fuel in China and many less developed countries. The smoke and pollution from older stoves attack the lungs and cause many deaths and illnesses each year. Today, aid agencies are trying to introduce simple clean coal stoves that burn more efficiently and give off less damaging smoke.

Coal soap

Pitch

Coal Products

- Coal is also used to produce detergents, fertilisers and explosives.
- Activated carbon from coal is used in air and water filters and in kidney dialysis machines.
- When bituminous coal is heated to make coke, it gives off gases. These are collected and cool into a liquid called coal tar, which can be used to make soaps or paints.
- Coal tar is used as pitch on roofs or as creosote to protect wood. The ash can be made into building blocks.
- Carbon fibre is also made from coal, an extremely strong but light material used in construction, cars, mountain bikes and tennis rackets.

Creosote

Gas from Coal

It is possible to produce gas from coal by heating it to very high temperatures away from air. In the Lurgi process, crushed coal is mixed with steam and pure oxygen to either create natural gas or synthetic gas – a mixture of carbon monoxide and hydrogen (which can also be used in fuel cells).

The advantage of turning coal to gas is that pollutants such as sulphur and ammonia can easily be extracted, creating a fuel that burns much more cleanly.

Synthetic Gas

Synthetic gas can be burnt in a power plant to turn a turbine and generate electricity. It can also be converted into transport fuels, like petrol, and plastics. In countries that have no oil or gas reserves, such as South Africa and the Czech Republic, converting coal to gas or petrol reduces their reliance on imports.

ENERGY FACTS: Town Gas

In the early 1800s, town gas was produced by burning coal. This gas was then burnt in street lamps. Later, town gas was also used for cooking and heating until it was replaced by natural gas in the 1960s.

◗ **Coal Gasification Plant** in Vresová, Czech Republic. This processes 5,000 tonnes of brown coal every day. The synthetic gas created is used to produce chemicals and fuel for power stations.

⚙ Gasification

The Lurgi process can be used to turn coal into natural gas (methane):

1 Coal is fed into a gasifier and turned to hydrogen and carbon monoxide by burning it with steam and oxygen.

2 The gas is cooled in a scrubber and condensed tars are removed.

3 Sulphur and ammonia are extracted, cleaning the gas.

4 Placed under great pressure at over 1600 ºC, the hydrogen and carbon dioxide react, forming methane and water vapour.

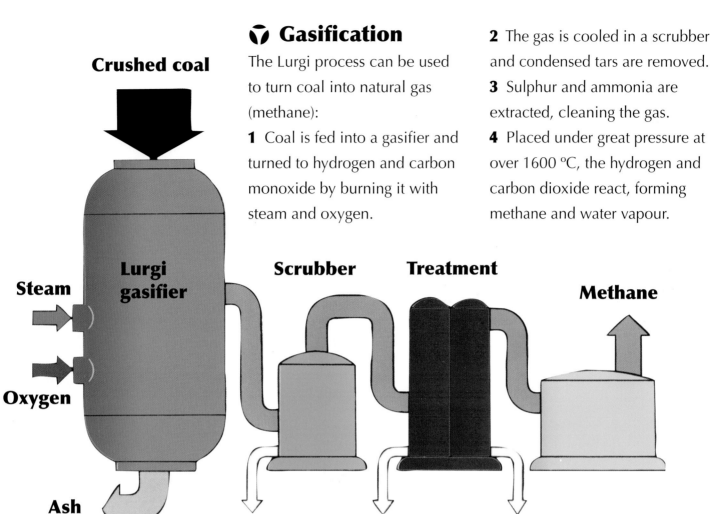

Crushed coal

Steam

Oxygen

Lurgi gasifier

Ash

Scrubber

Treatment

Methane

Tar and tar oils   Ammonia   Sulphur

Coal The Polluter

Coal deserves its reputation as a dirty fuel. Mining coal causes lots of dust and noise. It can leave giant mounds of waste, also known as slag, or huge scars on the land. Burning coal is a major contributor to global warming. Harmful gases are also released by coal-fired power stations and factories, causing suffocating smog. These gases mix with water in the clouds to form acid rain. A typical coal plant also sucks in billions of litres of cooling water, harming local habitats and wildlife.

Smog

In the past, when most homes used coal, London and other large cities suffered from terrible smogs. As a result, many cities have been made into smokeless zones. Factories that burn a lot of coal need to have efficient filtering and washing processes to cut down on the soot which enters the air.

♥ Acid Rain

The waste gases released by coal-burning power stations, including the gases sulphur and nitrogen, drift high into the atmosphere and dissolve in the water droplets of clouds. This water falls as acid rain, which pollutes lakes and rivers, kills plants and wildlife, and damages buildings. Winds can carry acid rain thousands of kilometres.

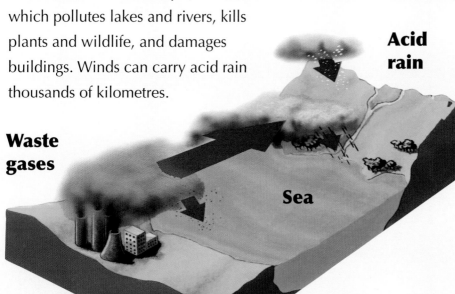

Waste gases

Acid rain

Sea

◬ Open-cast Destruction

Open-cast mines can destroy the landscape. Exhausted mines are sometimes converted to landfills and filled with solid waste, but many others are simply abandoned.

Sunlight

Trapped heat

Polluting gases

Rising sea levels

◬ Global Warming

More than any other fuel, coal releases carbon dioxide when it burns. This gas traps the Sun's heat and pushes up temperatures. Most scientists predict this global warming will make sea levels rise (due to polar ice caps melting) and bring extreme weather conditions including floods, storms and droughts.

Slag Heaps

Millions of tonnes of ash, sludge and toxic chemicals can sometimes be left after the coal has been sorted and cleaned, forming slag heaps.

Radiation Risk

Recent studies show that coal-fired power plants may release more radiation than nuclear power stations.

A Role for Coal?

ENERGY FACTS: Global Coal

- Coal is found on every continent in the world.
- Around 70 countries mine coal. Unless it is very poor quality or very hard to get at, it is mined.
- The two leading coal producers are China and the United States. Between them, they extract half of the coal mined in the world.
- In India, almost 70 per cent of carbon dioxide emissions are produced by burning coal.
- World coal use is expected to increase from 7 billion to nearly 9 billion tonnes by 2030.
- Coal use now accounts for around 20 per cent of the world's total greenhouse gas emissions.

Cheap and plentiful, coal will be an important source of energy for years to come. But it has yet to shed its dirty image. During the 1990s, the coal industry in the United States and Europe invested in new technology to tackle the release of sulphur and nitrogen oxides that cause acid rain. But the problem of carbon dioxide emissions remains.

Many environmental groups would prefer to see a mix of cleaner fossil fuels such as gas, more renewables, and greater energy efficiency. Meanwhile, the coal industry promises a new era of "clean" coal, arguing that new technology will allow power plants to burn coal more efficiently and store the carbon dioxide given off underground.

The Growth of Coal

Many experts predict that supplies of oil may soon peak. It's one reason why many countries, including China, India and Russia, are all using more coal to create electricity. In China, at the peak of its building programme in 2006, the equivalent of two large coal-fired power plants were completed every week. These new plants alone added 5 per cent to the world's carbon dioxide emissions.

◗ New Technology

The next generation of coal-fired power stations could cut carbon dioxide emissions by 40 per cent, but is it enough?

◖ The Human Cost

Mining has always been a dangerous job and though conditions for miners have improved in Europe and North America, many hazards remain. In 2007, an explosion 1,000 m down in the Zasyadko coal mine in Ukraine killed 80 miners, while another methane gas explosion killed 17 miners in 2009 at the Wojek coal mine in Poland.

Many Chinese coal mines are illegal and getting coal out is often more important than workers' lives. On 15 June 2009, the Xinqiao mine in southwestern China suddenly flooded, trapping 16 miners. Amazingly, three of them survived for 25 days by eating coal dust and licking water off the walls of the mine.

◖ Untapped Sources of Coal

With energy use on the rise, the search for more coal goes on all the time. Coal reserves that are difficult to mine can be exploited by converting the coal to gas while it is still underground. So far, the technology has only been used to mine shallow onshore coal deposits. In the future, it could be used to exploit some 3 trillion tonnes of coal lying under the seabed off the coast of Norway, a huge reserve that could provide the world with coal for an extra 50 years.

◖ Turning Coal into Gas

1 *One platform drills down into a seam to inject oxygen and water – this is often enough to set alight the coal which is under pressure at depth.*
2 *By controlling the amount of air pumped in, the coal only partly burns.*
3 *The gas given off is pumped up to another platform nearby, where it is converted to synthetic gas (syngas).*
4 *The processing platform will also need to filter out the carbon dioxide given off by gasification, and pump it back underground to store it.*

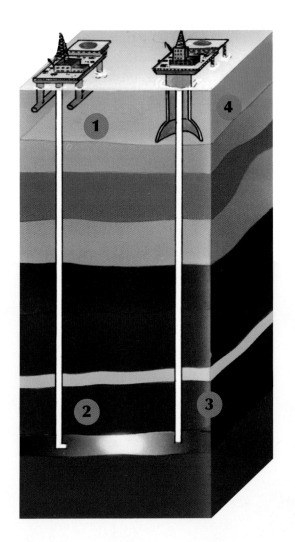

More Efficient Plants

China leads the world in building more efficient power plants. These burn less coal and emit less carbon dioxide for each unit of electricity they generate. By law, Chinese power companies must also retire an older, more polluting power plant for each new one they build.

Combined heat and power plants could also cut global warming emissions by more than a third compared with older plants. In the future, efficiency could be increased further by burning the coal at even higher temperatures in "supercritical turbines".

◑ The New Breed

China is growing at an incredible rate. The city of Shanghai alone gobbles up an extra 1,000 MW in power every year – about the same as the output from this new coal-fired plant at Waigaoqiao, Shanghai.

◑ Better Controls

Advanced measuring tools can boost the efficiency of coal-fired power plants. One laser-based device analyses the coal particles inside a boiler and automatically adjusts how the coal is being burnt, creating more power. It can also help to reduce the amount of pollutants and greenhouse gases being given off.

In the Lab
Developing laser measuring devices

Combined Heat and Power (CHP)

Conventional power plants that burn coal to make electricity release the heat into the air. Combined heat and power (CHP) plants have a steam turbine which not only drives a generator, but also produces hot water or steam.

Though very efficient, CHP plants are best suited to regions with long cold winters, such as Scandinavia and eastern Europe, where the heat is needed for several months a year.

Supercritical Turbines

The next generation of turbines will be able to operate with steam heated to 700 ºC and at very high pressures. For the same electricity supply, they consume 40 per cent less coal.

Some firms are now developing super-strength steel that will be able to withstand such high pressures and temperatures for many years. In older plants, the strength of the boiler decreases when used for long periods of time.

Not So Thirsty Power Plant

A typical 500-MW coal-fired power plant sucks in around 8 billion litres of water each year from nearby lakes or rivers to create steam for its turbines. That's enough water to support a city of roughly 250,000 people.

However, a coal-fired power plant has been built in the Australian outback that operates with just 10 per cent of the water used by a typical plant. By means of a special air-cooled condenser, the plant uses air instead of water to cool the hot steam from the plant turbine. This technology could be used to reduce the water used by coal-fired power plants in other areas.

Clean Coal?

⚠ Test Scrubbers

A German firm is developing a process that will remove most of the carbon dioxide released by burning coal by scrubbing it with special chemicals.

Clean coal technology (CCT) is already used to reduce pollution: electric air filters remove dust, fabric filters collect larger particles by sieving and limestone scrubbers remove harmful gases such as sulphur dioxide.

However, the future of coal depends more on finding a cheap and efficient way of capturing and storing carbon dioxide. In Florida, coal is being "cooked" to produce clean-burning gas; in Germany, carbon dioxide is being captured by scrubbers in the chimney and turned to liquid; and in the Sahara the gas is being pumped into desert rocks. If carbon capture works, then King Coal will be around for a long time.

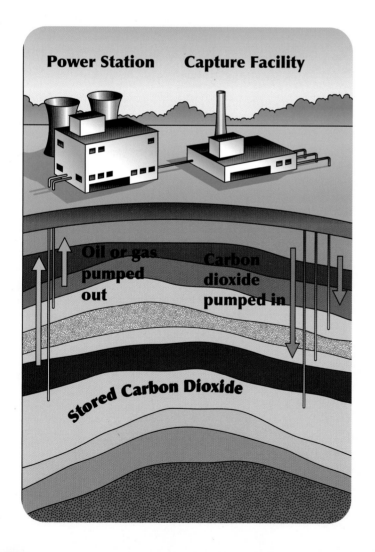

◁ Carbon Capture

It is hoped that carbon capture and storage (CCS) will catch and remove carbon dioxide and store it underground, preventing this greenhouse gas from entering the atmosphere, where it contributes to global warming.

The carbon dioxide could be stored in various locations:

1 *Pumped into disused coal fields replacing the methane which can be used as fuel.*

2 *Pumped and dissolved into salty underwater reservoirs, known as aquifers.*

3 *Pumped along existing pipelines into older oil fields where it will help to maintain the pressure, making it easier to extract the oil (see diagram, left).*

4 *Dissolved in deep sea water, though this could make the oceans more acidic, harming wildlife.*

Clean Coal Technology

The sulphur dioxide that causes acid rain can be removed by spraying a mixture of limestone and water over the waste gases in a coal-burning plant or factory. Known as "wet scrubbers", these can be over 95 per cent effective. The mixture reacts with the sulphur dioxide to form gypsum, which can be used to make building materials.

Toxic nitrogen oxide can be reduced using specially-designed "low NOx" burners that restrict the amount of oxygen available in the hottest part of the boiler where the coal is burned.

▼ Oxyfuel Process

Some of the latest power stations (see below) burn coal in pure oxygen instead of air (which is 78 per cent nitrogen). This prevents large amounts of nitrogen turning into nitrogen oxides during combustion, so that the waste gas is made mostly of carbon dioxide and water vapour.

By cooling and condensing the water, the carbon dioxide can then be separated and stored underground.

Algae Farm

▶ Coal, Biofuels and Algae

In some plants, biofuels such as wood chips and coal are burned in the same furnace. This can reduce the amount of greenhouse gases and pollutants such as sulphur dioxide.

In the future, algae farms may also be built alongside power stations. Algae can eat just about anything in order to produce fats in their body that can be turned into biofuels, including the carbon dioxide and nitrogen dioxide released by coal-fired power plants.

HOT OFF THE PRESS

Coal Gasification Test Sites in the UK

■ There may be five times as much coal below the sea or very deep underground as there is nearer to the surface where it can be easily mined. This coal can still be turned into fuel by burning it underground and capturing the gas given off.

New technology that does this is now being tested at five offshore sites around the British coast, the first of which is in Swansea Bay in Wales. If things go well, a full-scale operation could be up and running by 2014.

Swansea Bay, Wales – a test site for coal gasification

However, the firm behind the project still has to find an effective way of capturing the other gas produced by the process – carbon dioxide.

Low-NOx Burners

■ Along with sulphur, the nitrogen oxide (NOx) released by burning coal is one of the major causes of acid rain and smog. This gas can also be harmful to health, irritating the throat, lungs and eyes.

In the future, however, Low-NOx burners could help coal-fired plants to reduce nitrogen oxide emissions by up to 40 per cent. These specially-designed burners restrict the amount of oxygen available in the hottest part of the furnace where the coal is burned.

First US Carbon Capture Test Site

■ The United States is planning its first large-scale coal-fired plant fitted with carbon capture technology, known as the FutureGen project. Eventually it is hoped that the plant will capture up to 90 per cent of the carbon dioxide given off, or one million tonnes each year. The plant will generate 275 MW of electricity, enough to power around 150,000 US homes.

Carbon capture technology being developed in Germany

Direct Carbon Fuel Cells

■ Scientists have recently come up with a way to create twice as much power from coal while reducing the amount of carbon dioxide released by 50 per cent.

The Direct Carbon Fuel Cell (DCFC) will convert coal to electricity directly, rather than burning it to boil water into steam that turns a turbine. No burning is required, no water is used in the process, and DCFCs could be built as small, local plants or grouped to form large power stations.

How does it work?

DCFCs have a core of ceramic tubes. Inside these, carbon in the coal is gasified into carbon monoxide. When this gas mixes with oxygen at 900 °C, electricity is created while giving off a pure stream of carbon dioxide. Ash, sulphur, lead, and other wastes are not released into the air but put in landfills or recycled.

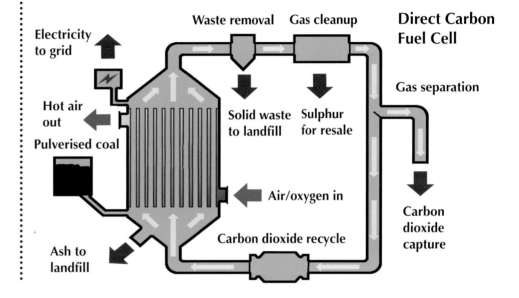

A Source of Hydrogen?

■ Using gasifiers to turn coal into gas could one day also provide a source of hydrogen. This gas could either be fed back into a power plant as an extra fuel, or used in fuel cells.

Fuel cells convert energy from chemical reactions between oxygen and hydrogen directly into electricity. They are already used to supply power to cars, hospitals and spacecraft.

This German submarine is powered by fuel cells.

From Coal to Plastic

■ Most plastics are made from oil. In the last two years, however, China has built nearly 20 plants that convert coal into a gas that can be used to make plastics and medicines.

This process happens on an enormous scale – one factory has five giant gasifiers for turning coal into gas, each 18 m tall and weighing over 220 tonnes.

How Coal Compares

While coal and other fossil fuels are cheap, they release carbon dioxide into the atmosphere, causing pollution and global warming. Wind power and other forms of renewable energy will reduce this problem, but may only be able to supply 20 per cent of our energy needs. Nuclear power could provide us with the extra power, but reactors are expensive and take years to build.

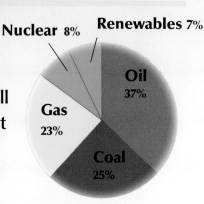

Nuclear 8% **Renewables** 7%

Oil 37%

Gas 23%

Coal 25%

NON-RENEWABLE ENERGY

World Energy Sources

Coal

For:
Coal is cheap and supplies of coal are expected to last another 150 years.

Against:
Coal-fired power stations give off the most greenhouse gases. They also produce sulphur dioxide, creating acid rain. Coal mining can be very destructive to the landscape.

Gas

For:
Gas is relatively cheap, and produces less greenhouses gases than oil and coal.

Against:
Burning gas releases carbon dioxide. Gas is not renewable and the world's natural gas reserves are limited. Gas pipelines can disrupt the migration routes of animals such as caribou.

Oil

For:
Oil is cheap and easy to store, transport and use.

Against:
Oil is not renewable and it is getting more expensive to get out of the ground. Burning oil releases large amounts of greenhouse gases. Oil spills, especially at sea, cause severe pollution.

Nuclear

For:
Nuclear power is constant and reliable, and doesn't contribute to global warming.

Against:
Not renewable as uranium (the main nuclear fuel) will eventually run out. Nuclear waste is so dangerous it must be buried for thousands of years. Also the risk of a nuclear accident.

RENEWABLE ENERGY

Solar Power

For:

Solar power needs no fuel, it's renewable and doesn't pollute.

Against:

Solar power stations are very expensive as solar (photovoltaic) cells cost a lot compared to the amount of electricity they produce. They're unreliable unless used in a very sunny climate.

Wind Power

For:

Wind power needs no fuel, it's renewable and doesn't pollute.

Against:

Wind is unpredictable, so wind farms need a back-up power supply. Possible danger to bird flocks. It takes thousands of wind turbines to produce the same power as a nuclear plant.

Hydroelectric Power

For:

Hydroelectric power needs no fuel, is renewable and doesn't pollute.

Against:

Hydro-electric is very expensive to build. A large dam will flood a very large area upstream, impacting on animals and people there. A dam can affect water quality downstream.

Geothermal Power

For:

Geothermal power needs no fuel, it's renewable and doesn't pollute.

Against:

There aren't many suitable places for a geothermal power station as you need hot rocks of the right type and not too deep. It can "run out of steam". Underground poisonous gases can be a danger.

Biofuels

For:

Biofuels are cheap and renewable and can be made from waste.

Against:

Growing biofuels from energy crops reduces the land available for food and uses up vital resources such as fresh water. Like fossil fuels, biofuels can produce greenhouse gases.

Tidal Power

For:

Tidal power needs no fuel, is reliable, renewable and doesn't pollute.

Against:

Tidal power machines are expensive to build and only provide power for around 10 hours each day, when the tide is actually moving in or out. Not an efficient way of producing electricity.

Glossary and Resources

acid rain Rain that has become acidic after mixing with sulphur, nitrogen and other gases released into the atmosphere, often caused by burning fossil fuels such as coal in large power stations.

carbon capture Capturing carbon dioxide and storing it underground.

clean coal technologies (CCT) Burning coal in a cleaner, more efficient way, such as scrubbing and gasification.

coal field A region with large reserves of coal ready to be extracted.

coke Almost pure carbon, made by heating coal to a very high temperature without air. Used to manufacture steel.

extract To take something out.

fossil fuel A fuel such as coal, oil or gas that is formed underground from the remains of prehistoric plants and animals.

furnace A chamber used to burn fuel at a high temperature.

gasification Turning solid fuels such as coal into a gas by partly burning them.

generator A machine that turns the energy of a moving object into electricity.

geologist A scientist who studies the Earth.

global warming A warming of the Earth's surface. Many scientists predict that global warming may lead to more floods, droughts and rising sea levels.

greenhouse effect The global warming caused by human-made gases, such as carbon dioxide and methane, that trap the heat from the Sun in the atmosphere.

megawatt (MW) A million watts (a watt is a unit of power). A gigawatt is 1,000 MW.

national grid A country's network of electric power lines.

offshore At sea, not far from the coast.

open-cast mining Mining by making a large hole at the surface rather than tunnelling underground. Also known as strip mining.

precipitator A machine that collects particles of dust from coal smoke.

pulverise To crush into tiny pieces.

radiation Energy (sometimes toxic) given out in waves by high-energy particles.

renewable Something that can be used over and over without running out.

scrubbing Using chemicals or filters to remove sulphur when coal is being burnt.

smelting A process that separates a metal from its ore (the rock that contains it).

smog A polluting mix of fog and smoke.

syngas Synthetic gas made from coal, a mix of hydrogen and carbon monoxide.

turbine A machine with rotating blades.

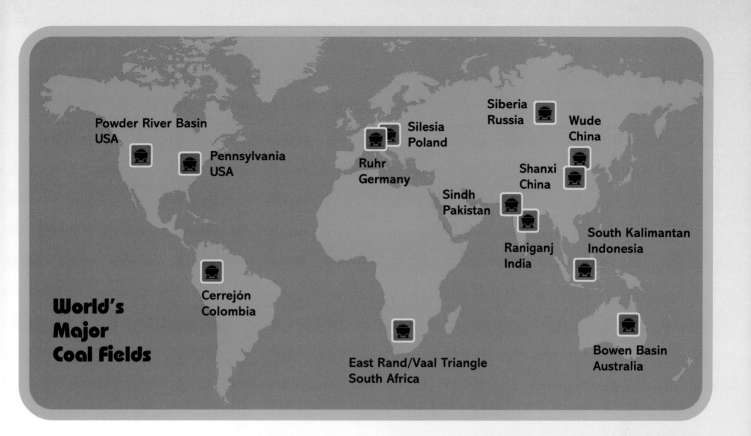

World's Major Coal Fields

- Powder River Basin USA
- Pennsylvania USA
- Cerrejón Colombia
- Ruhr Germany
- Silesia Poland
- Sindh Pakistan
- Siberia Russia
- Wude China
- Shanxi China
- Raniganj India
- South Kalimantan Indonesia
- East Rand/Vaal Triangle South Africa
- Bowen Basin Australia

Useful Websites

If you're interested in finding out more about coal and coal mining, the following websites are helpful:

www.tonto.eia.doe.gov/kids/energy
www.nma.org
www.bhpbilliton.com
www.cmhrc.co.uk/site/home
www.bbc.co.uk/wales/history/sites/
    themes/industry.shtml
www.teachcoal.org/

ENERGY FACTS:
Top Ten Coal Producing Countries

The ten countries producing the most coal in 2008 were:

1 **China** – 2,761 million tonnes
2 **United States** – 1007 million tonnes
3 **India** – 490 million tonnes
4 **Australia** – 325 million tonnes
5 **Russia** – 247 million tonnes
6 **Indonesia** – 246 million tonnes
7 **South Africa** – 236 million tonnes
8 **Kazakhstan** – 104 million tonnes
9 **Poland** – 84 million tonnes
10 **Colombia** – 79 million tonnes

Further reading

World Issues: Energy Crisis by Ewan McLeish (Aladdin/Watts)
Our World: Coal by Kate Bedford (Aladdin/Watts)
Energy Sources: Fossil Fuels by Neil Morris (Franklin Watts)
Energy Today: Oil, Gas and Coal by Tea Benduhn (Gareth Stevens Publishing)
Energy Debate: Coal, Gas, and Oil by Sally Morgan (Rosen Central)
Issues in Our World: Energy Crisis by Ewan McLeish (Aladdin/Watts)

Index

Photocredits

(Abbreviations: t – top, m – middle, b – bottom, l – left, r – right).

All photos istockphoto.com except: 3tl, 16-17b, 20bl, 22-23 all, 24tl, 25t, 26bl: Siemens GmbH. 3b: Velvetweb / Dreamstime.com. 4-5: Pillbox / Dreamstime.com. 6tl: Diebar / Dreamstime.com. 8tl: Kinlem / Dreamstime.com. 11b, 16tl: US Department of Energy. 14tl: NASA. 25br: Valcent Products Inc.